FOUR SEASONS IN THE NORTH

by
Hunter Adair

HUTTON PRESS
1997

Published by the Hutton Press Ltd.,
130 Canada Drive, Cherry Burton, Beverley,
East Yorkshire, HU17 7SB

Printed and bound by
Clifford Ward & Co. (Bridlington) Ltd.,
55 West street, Bridlington, East Yorkshire,
YO15 3DZ

ISBN 1 872167 91 8

CONTENTS

SWALLOWS
IN FLIGHT

INTRODUCTION

The four seasons in the north of England and in some parts of Scotland, are very much different from other parts of the country. The seasons are at least two or three weeks behind other parts of the country, and it is much colder in the north than it is in the south, although the seasons have been changing in the north over these past ten years.

If the spring of the year is cold and wet, then the rest of the year can be late in coming. The April of 1992 was a terribly wet month in the north. Sheep and lambs died on many hill and lowland farms. We had heavy falls of snow on the hills, along with heavy rain and strong winds altogether, and sheep just can't stand that sort of punishment.

However a good summer can soon repair the damage to the countryside made by a bad spring. Wild birds and animals bring up their families in a flurry of activity and the flowers and fauna are normally in full bloom. Visitors start arriving in the north from all over the world to visit some of the beautiful coastline in the north and to visit sites, such as the Roman Wall in Northumberland, or to the Lake District in Cumbria.

The autumn is a lovely time of year in the north. The changing colours of many trees and plants are delightful to see. The swallows, sand martins and the cuckoo are all thinking about heading back to Africa, while the curlews start leaving the hills and moors to the grouse, while they spend the winter on the coast.

The winters in the north have been changing over these past ten years. They have been much milder and there has been very little snow over the past few years worth talking about. I can remember in the 'sixties and the 'seventies, we had some very very hard winters in the north, with deep falls of snow and some very hard frosts. The frosts some nights were as hard as -7 or -9 degrees at times. The very hard severe weather killed off many birds and animals due to starvation. But the winter still showed its beauty in many shapes and forms.

The photographs are all about what the reader can see throughout the four seasons in the countryside: the trees, shrubs, wild flowers, birds, wild animals and some domestic farm animals. The photographs also show some people that live and work in the countryside. It is hoped the book will be a useful guide for the many children and adults who visit the countryside all the year round, as well as a keepsake for visitors.

Gundogs

SPRING

A rookery which is used every year by rooks. The nests are repaired before the birds sit. The young rooks are normally sitting out on the tree branches by the middle of May.

Rooks at the nests. The rook is the only large black bird with a bare face patch. They also have baggy thigh feathers.

The lapwing, or the peewit, by which it is better known to most country people, is quite easy to recognise by its black and white appearance. Its back has a green tint in sunlight. In flight it calls 'peewit'. Likes farmland, moor, bog and coastal areas.

The redshank is the only wading bird with a broad white hindwing, which can be seen when the bird is in flight. It has a grey brown plumage when it's at rest. Has orange-red legs and bill. Frequents moors, bogs, marshland and coastal areas.

A small group of snowdrops in the early Spring. The rootstocks of the snowdrops are little brown bulbs.

The flowering catkin which is a waterside tree. The catkins appear before the leaves to facilitate pollination by the wind.

A small drooping willow tree in flower.

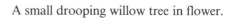

A horse chestnut tree in flower.

10

A pair of young lambs in the Spring of the year.

Jacob sheep are very attractive. The lambs are a distinctive black and white, they change colour to brown and white as they get older. They have either four or six horns, or they are polled.

11

A ewe casting her coat in the Spring before the wool is clipped from her.

A Swaledale Tup sitting on top of a rock. The breed takes its name from the valley of the River Swale in Yorkshire. The breed is alert and of a reasonable size to suit the moorland environment.

A view of a house in the Lake District when the mist was coming down from the hills.

Groups of narcissus and daffodils growing along a hedge bottom. They bring colour to the countryside in the Spring.

13

Spring flowers in front of an old mangle.

Spring crocus flowers in Hexham Park in Northumberland.

Spring flowers in one of Hull's streets. Hull fountain garden display, close to Queens Gardens. The Town Docks Museum is in the background.

A group of narcissus which flower in the Spring of the year between March and April.

A young calf only a few days old being sold in the cattle ring.

A young calf only a few days old, with a white face. This is a cross-bred calf between a Hereford and a Friesian.

Cattle waggons unloading at Hexham cattle market. The market is open at least two days a week.

A mother and calf being sold together in the market ring.

The floor of the wood is covered with the broad, bright-green pointed leaves and the white flowers of the wild garlic.

The white starlike flowers of the wild garlic. If the stem of the plant is crushed it has a pungent smell of onions.

This handsome plant of the countryside, the willow-herb, grows about one metre high and likes light soil. It grows along hedgerows and in fairly open woods. The willow-herb produces a large rosy purple flower.

Two young girls with their ponies demonstrating the dressage movements at Bishop Burton College of Agriculture at Beverley in East Yorkshire.

An alder bush beside a river with its green leaves in the Spring of the year. The bush is then attacked by a particular type of caterpillar which eats all the leaves of the bush.

The same alder bush after it has been attacked by the caterpillars. The bush is covered in webs which the caterpillars make to protect themselves from birds and other predators.

A close up of a web on the alder bush which may have many caterpillars in it eating the bush leaves. Once the caterpillars pupate, the bush usually recovers and puts on new leaves.

Three stages of the dandelions which grow in fields, pastures and in many waste places.

The flowers of the blackthorn, or sloe which appear in full bloom between March and April. The whole bush is covered with white flowers which look like snow.

The black fruit of the sloe have a velvet appearance when they are ready for picking. The fruit is slightly bitter to taste.

The rich colour of the sloe-gin made by the author. This is how to make it. Take one cup of sloes, prick with a fork. Add one cup of sugar, put into a bottle and then add a bottle of Gin. Leave for two or three months, then filter the liquid.

The orange-red hips of the wild rose are nut shaped fruit and are used in the manufacture of Rose-hip Syrup, which is very rich in vitamin C.

Grass which is cut for silage can be stored in a clamp and is covered with plastic sheeting to seal it, which helps the fermentation. The silage is used as winter feed for cattle and sheep.

Silage can also be wrapped in black plastic sheeting, or stored in plastic bags.

Grass which is cut and dried for hay can also be wrapped with a net and made into big bales. Hay is used to feed a variety of farm and domestic animals.

Mr. William Oliver, showing members of The Institute of Bankers from Newcastle-upon-Tyne around his farm and parts of the Roman Wall, where he farms in South Northumberland.

25

SUMMER

A tree trunk lying in a field which has been decaying for many years.

An evergreen Rhododendron flowering shrub with a twisted stem.

A broken silver birch tree with some fungi growing on the trunk.

Belsay Hall Quarry Gardens in Northumberland.

The foxglove is one of the best known flowers of the countryside with its purple, or white flowers. A bee enters the flower of the foxglove, the hairs on its body brush up the pollen and convey it to the stigma of an old flower.

A familiar mass of purple and white blossom of the foxglove. They grow where timber has been cut down and on many dry waste areas of land.

A spear-plume thistle which flowers from July to October. It grows on farmland, in rough pastures and on many uncultivated areas of land.

Wild goats on the Galloway Hills in Scotland. They are not always easily seen.

The red berries of the cuckoo-pint plant, which is quite common throughout the country. It is also known as "Lords-and-Ladies" and can be found in woods and along hedgerows.

The wild honeysuckle is one of our most familiar flowers. It is a very popular flower because of its beauty and for its powerful scent. It is also very rich in nectar. It can be found in woods and along hedgerows.

The woodcock sitting among some cover in the summer. They are stout built little birds with large eyes and a long beak. They measure about 355mm from bill to tail and weigh about 330g.

The beautiful purple and white flower head of the Rhododendron bush. It also has ever-green leaves.

The Haydon Fox Hounds in Northumberland, out for their morning exercise. During the summer the morning's walk can cover several miles.

Divers returning from the beach on the Northumberland coast.

Timber being loaded on the road-side by a self-loading waggon in Northumberland.

Some goats will sit anywhere. This goat in Northumberland seems to be quite happy sitting on top of a Ford car.

A white and pied wagtail sitting on top of a stone wall. It is the only black and white bird of its size with a long tail. The wagtail can be found on farmland, in woods and in domestic gardens.

Brambles changing colour during the summer from green, red, to black, or purple. The fruit is sweet when ripe and is used for making jams, jellies and tarts.

The red berries of the hawthorn, which is one of the commonest trees in the British Isles, and which makes good hedgerows. The fruit is very popular with a variety of wild birds in the winter.

A stone-built tunnel which once supplied air to one of the lead mines in Northumberland. There were normally several air tunnels to a mine.

A farmer with one of his pedigree Ayrshire cows. The breed was developed in Scotland and was bred to produce milk. The cows produce good quality milk with about 4 per cent butterfat.

A farmer from Cumbria feeding his black and white Friesian cows with hay during the very dry summer of 1989, when many farmers were short of grass.

A young Jersey cow. They are quite a small breed of cattle and are bred to produce milk. The cows produce a very good rich quality milk.

A young Hereford cow with horns. Some of the breed have horns and some are polled. The Hereford cattle are bred for beef and they cross well with some dairy breeds.

A young girl on her way to the beach in Northumberland, sits on a gate to have her photograph taken.

Young children playing at a field water trough where cattle and sheep drink.

A young boy with his pet ducks on a
Cumbrian farm.

Children out in a country lane with
their friends and ponies.

A Clydesdale horse being washed down with a hose pipe getting it ready for the show ring at the Royal Highland Show in Edinburgh.

A young Clydesdale horse having its legs rubbed down with sawdust, after its legs have been washed, and before it goes into the show ring.

Mr. John Dodd from Langley-on-Tyne in Northumberland putting out heaps of animal manure with one of his Clydesdale horses and box cart. The manure is later spread with a hand fork.

This was a famous Clydesdale stallion called 'Baron of Buchlyvie'. There was a dispute over the ownership of the stallion, which went to the House of Lords at the end of 1911. The stallion was sold at auction in Ayr cattle market in Scotland for a world record price of £9,500.

A Limousin bull which is used in this country mainly to cross breed with our native cattle for beef, although there are also a number of pedigree Charolais herds in this country.

A lady and gentleman out walking their dogs in Hexham Woods. It is very good exercise for both owners and dogs.

A pen of Limousin bullocks at Bishop Burton College of Agriculture at Beverley in East Yorkshire.

A selection of the farm stand which was part of the Gateshead Garden Festival held in Co. Durham during the summer of 1990.

Neil Milbourne from Crosby-on-Eden at Carlisle with young nephew and niece and two Labrador puppies.

The author's wife (centre) at Galloway in Scotland, collecting a young pedigree Springer spaniel pup from friends who bred the dog.

Richard Adair preparing a barbecue for the family at Middle Shield farm in Hexham, Northumberland.

Sitting at his desk Mr. Alan Collett, the Estate Manager for the Hetton Steads Estate in North Northumberland.

The badger is a nocturnal animal and is spread throughout the country. At one time badger grease was used as an excellent cure for wounds. The hair was used for making paint and shaving brushes and in some places, the hams of the badgers were eaten. The badger is thankfully now a protected species.

Mr. John Hankie and his family from Esh Hall, Esh Village in Co. Durham. Members of the Hankie family have lived at Esh Hall since about 1904.

Building a drystone wall. Many farm and moor walls are built to a height of 4ft 6ins. (1.37m) to the coping, or capping stone, which is the top stone on the wall top.

The centre of drystone walls are filled with small packing stones and for every running yard (0.91m) of farm, or moor wall built, there is roughly a good ton of stone used.

Stone walls have many features. This wall has a hole at the base to let surface water pass through it. There are also stones sticking out of the wall. These are known as 'through stones' or 'thrusts', which help to stabilise the wall.

This stone-built lime kiln on a Northumberland farm was never used. It was left to flood and has developed into a nice pond for wildlife.

A stone wall with a hole at the base. This hole is to let sheep pass from one pasture to another and has many names, such as 'sheep run, smout hole, lunky hole, sheep smoose, cripple hole' or 'thirl hole'.

A red admiral butterfly drops onto a thistle.

The red berries of the viburnum opulus plant which grows along hedgerows and in other uncultivated scrub areas.

The purple-black cherries of the elder hang in clusters and are used by many people for making wine and jelly.

The floor of the wood is covered with bluebells, which is a common woodland plant throughout Britain. The flowers appear in the spring and can go right through to the early autumn.

Ferns in a wood changing colour in the early autumn.

Mr. Jack Lowes from Nebrough, near Hexham, in Northumberland. Jack makes and teaches the art of stick dressing. The walking stick with the carved trout took 100 hours to make.

A farmer in Cumbria outside a stone building which was once used as a dry toilet.

The red grouse which is Britain's hardiest bird. It lives on the heather hills and moors all the year round. It eats the shoots of young heathers.

A long steel 12ft. (3.65m) pole which was used on the moors to tell how far the rock lay under the peat.

A crop of standing oats which are very much different from barley and wheat, as the grain on the oats grows from branches on the main stalk. The branches can be three inches (75mm) apart and the grain spikelets hang from the branches.

A combine harvester cutting, threshing and loading a trailer with barley, which is mainly used for stock feed.

A standing crop of wheat which is used for making bread. The ear of the wheat grows on notches on the main stalk and wheat has no branches like corn.

A farm manager standing in a field of barley. He has some wheat in his right hand and barley in his left hand. Barley is the crop which has the long beard.

Three generations of the Wilson family, who farm at Charlesfield Farm near the Scottish border.

Creamery staff and milk tanker drivers at a milk factory at Newcastle-upon-Tyne.

Auctioneers selling a land roller at a farm stock and machinery sale in South Northumberland.

Mr. John Hubbock and his secretary Chris. John is an agricultural merchant in the Hexham area. He has been in the business for many years and provides a good service to the farmers.

A grey heron standing on a stone in shallow water waiting for fish or frogs to pass by.

A beech tree changing colour in the autumn.

A roe buck grazing in a wood one autumn evening. Roe deer make play rings which might be round a big bush, or clump of trees. Cattle also have play areas in fields.

A weasel standing on its hind legs checking to see what had disturbed it.

An old threshing machine restored to working order. It was used on most farms throughout the country for threshing the corn sheaves before the combine harvester came along.

A small conference pear tree, which produces a very heavy crop of fruit nearly every year. The tree is about 20 years old.

A small apple tree which produces a nice crisp eating apple called Ellison Orange. The tree is about 25 years old.

On the east coast in Northumberland, at Amble, a race is held every year along part of the coast for running clubs and individuals. These are some of the runners in action.

61

A pair of heavy horses at a ploughing match in the North East.

An international vintage tractor at a ploughing match at Morpeth in Northumberland in 1987.

Adjusting the plough during a ploughing match in Northumberland in 1987.

Farmers visiting a farm in Cumbria looking at the bluefaced ewes and lambs.

Stone built farm buildings on a Cumbrian farm. Part of the building on the left with the wooden steps up into the building was where grain or hay were stored to feed the cattle in the winter.

A stone built grouse butt. On the wall top there are soil turfs which are put there to protect the wall, and where the grouse shooters can lay their guns without getting them scratched on the stone.

A typical country estate house, along the Scottish English border.

Netherby Estate House, at Longtown in Cumbria on the Scottish English border. The same family has owned the estate for generations.

A young cygnet has got lost from its family on the River Tyne at Newcastle.

Mr. Ian Sutherland (left) 1991 National Farmers' Union county chairman, in Northumberland, hands over to Mr. Nicholas White at the end of his term.

The kestrel often hunts methodically along the sides of the motorways, while the traffic is racing past at a very high speed. The kestrel will hover as low as five metres above the ground, and finding no prey at one particular spot, it will wheel and glide a short distance further along the motorway and there it will start to hover and hang in the air again.

Two pairs of Clydesdale horses ploughing stubble fields on a farm in the North East of England.

The Winterburn family from Heddon-on-the-Wall at Newcastle-upon-Tyne looking at their dairy herd of black and white Friesian cows which are housed for the winter.

High force waterfall at Middleton-in-Teesdale, in Barnard Castle, Co. Durham.

Two black and white Friesian dairy cows waiting their turn in the collecting yard, before going into the milking parlour to be milked.

Mr. John Hubbuck with one of his sons checking the quality of some hay. John has been an agricultural merchant in Hexham, Northumberland, for over 40 years.

The entrance to a stone field drain which can run right across the field. The drain is covered with soil and grass and the water from this drain runs into the river.

A robin standing among the snow covered grass. The robin was feeding on nuts, which were falling from a nut net hanging from a tree above.

A pair of cormorants fishing for eels in the raging water of the River Tyne at Hexham in Northumberland.

Woodland management being carried out in a hardwood in the North, to let the new younger trees grow and develop.

The late Mr. Eddie Armstrong from Wooley Park Farm in Allendale standing on top of a snow drift in 1963. The snow was several metres deep.

The author's springer spaniel dog retrieving a rabbit.

Two pointer dogs working on
the Durham Grouse Moor.

Pheasants being laid out and counted at the end of a pheasant drive.

A group of beaters on their way to the start of the next pheasant drive.

A group of shooters discussing the results of the previous drive.

A gamekeeper and his wife with their spaniel dogs collecting pheasants at the end of the drive.

A small brick built cowshed where the cows come in to be milked.
There is a glass sterile line above the cows which takes the milk direct into the farm dairy.

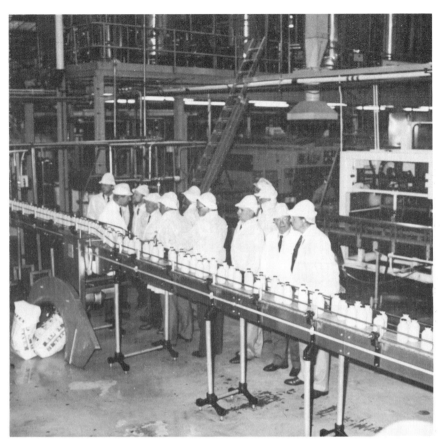

Farmers visiting a modern dairy factory in the north, where they are watching strawberry flavoured milk being bottled.

A dead silver birch tree with fungi growing out from the trunk.

Reflections of the silver birch trees in the River Tyne at Hexham, in Northumberland, during the month of January.

The acorns of the oak tree. The oak tree is recognisable by the rounded outline of its frame. Squirrels, mice and rats are all fond of acorns.

The fruit of the larch tree. The larch is a deciduous conifer, as it loses its leaves each year.

The trunk of a larch tree, which was introduced into England in the sixteenth century. Larch trees were first grown as ornamental trees, but are now used for their valuable timber.

Farmers at a sheep sale at Tyneside market in Newcastle-upon-Tyne.

Grouse in the North during a snow blizzard. When the weather is very hard with heavy falls of snow, the grouse will come right down near to towns and villages looking for food.

Mr. Willie Kilpatrick from Craigie Mains Farm, at Kilmarnock, Ayrshire in Scotland, washing a young Friesian bull, getting it ready for sale.

81

Mr. Batey from Haydon Bridge in Northumberland puts his milk into an orange emergency tank, because the road to his farm was blocked by snow and the collection vehicle could not get to his farm.

A modern milking parlour, where the cows stand behind one another to be milked.

A modern combine harvester which can soon cut and thresh a field of grain.

A milk tanker driver collecting milk from churns and plastic containers during a snow blizzard in the North.

83

The Fox